Native Legacy:
Indigenous Innovations and Contributions to the World

An Educational Resource for Middle Grade
Students and Above

Gary Robinson

Tribal Eye Productions
Santa Ynez, California

Copyright © 2019 GARY ROBINSON

ISBN 978-0-9800272-1-1

All rights reserved.

DEDICATION

*This book is dedicated to my best friend
and life partner, Lola, who inspires me
and reminds me of the important things in life.*

ACKNOWLEDGMENTS

I say "Wado" (Thank-you in Cherokee) to the many Native people I've met and known in my life—people who have taught me the values, perspectives and priorities I try to use in my everyday life.

-THE AUTHOR

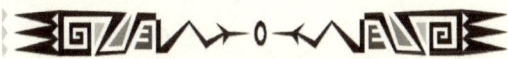

CONTENTS

1	Introduction	1
2	Food/Food Preparation	3
3	Mother Earth's Medicine	9
4	Other Useful Innovations	13
5	Political Concepts	17
6	Architectural Diversity	19
7	Transportation Routes	21
8	American Cities	23
9	Native Words and Place Names	25
10	Code Talkers & U.S. Victories	27
11	Indians, Animals & the Environment	29
12	Games and Sports	33
13	Bibliography	37

Introduction:
North American Achievements

The great achievements of North America in economics, politics, technology and agriculture are the result of the coming together of a richly diverse mixture of peoples and cultures. Beneath the surface of many of modern accomplishments lie indigenous origins.

The first European immigrants who settled in North America relied heavily on American Indian developments, techniques, lifestyles and perspectives in order to survive, and then thrive. In all areas of life including agriculture, hunting and fishing, housing, medicines, travel and others, European immigrants blended their civilization with American Indian civilizations, and together, they produced a unique hybrid society of unequaled achievement.

Euro-Americans have cleared the land, built large cities and made a nation, but haven't really taken the time to learn the story of <u>this</u> land. That story comes from the indigenous people who have lived upon it for thousands of years.

But the contributions and accomplishments made by Native Americans don't stop at the continental border. The ingenuity of the Indigenous Peoples of the Americas has impacted the entire world in ways that most modern planet-dwellers are totally unaware of.

Europeans and their descendants have been in the New World for centuries, but much of the original America, Indigenous America, has yet to really be discovered.

Note: Sources for the information presented in this book can be found in the bibliography at the end of the book.

Food and Food Production

Agricultural Techniques - Indians of the Americas developed over 300 food crops that exhibited a wide variety of sizes, textures, colors and growing conditions for the very practical need to insure that food sources would survive under a variety of conditions. They developed a method of freeze-drying vegetables in the mountains. They used cross-pollination and hybridization techniques to improve and strengthen plants. Some of these techniques were studied and adopted by European explorers and colonists. Many foods were ignored for long periods of time, only to be re-discovered and used by later generations. The French called corn and potatoes "miracle crops" because they grew abundantly and provided a cheap source of nutrition.

Colonial Survival - When English settlers first arrived in New England, they desperately needed food and turned to the Indians who supplied large quantities of meat, fish, nuts, berries and local vegetables. The early settlers had brought crops from England that would not grow in the American soil and climate.

The English settlers didn't know how to hunt because that was an activity that only royalty and nobility could undertake in their country. American Indians taught the colonists how to hunt and how to grow food. As the colonies spread and pushed the Indians back, and as European diseases killed off entire Indian villages, the colonists became known as "frontiersmen," using the skills they had learned from Native Americans.

Foods developed by Indians of the Americas - The list of foods developed by the Natives of the Americas is long and sometimes surprising. Some of these foods are commonly and erroneously thought to come from other places. Tomatoes, corn, potatoes, chili peppers (of all sizes, shapes and degrees of spiciness), various herbs & spices, wild rice, coffee, chocolate, peanuts, kidney beans, string beans, snap beans, lima beans, sunflowers, amaranth (the highest protein grain), vanilla and dried meat (jerky) are among the foods on this list.

Thanksgiving Day - While many Americans aren't aware of it, most of the traditional foods of a Thanksgiving feast are foods that American Indians taught the colonists how to find, catch, grow and prepare. These include: turkey, cornbread stuffing, cranberry sauce, succotash, corn, sweet potatoes, baked beans with maple syrup and pecan pie.

The Three Sisters (corn, beans and squash) - Many tribes knew that the secret of a healthy balanced vegetarian diet consisted of these three elements. When eaten together, they provide complete protein and plenty of fiber. When grown together in the fields, the wide corn leaves provide shade for the beans and squash, as well as providing a living stake for the bean vines to grow on.

Corn - First developed in the central valley of Mexico some 5,000 years ago and quickly spread to many indigenous nations in all corners of the Americas, corn was not widely accepted in Europe. It did however become very popular among the Euro-Americans in the South. Because wheat grew poorly in much of the South, corn was used as a dietary staple in many forms.

From American Indians, Southerners learned to enjoy corn on the cob, in succotash, ground into grits, popped as a snack and turned into hominy. It's most common use, however, was in the form of cornbread. The Southern dish known as "hush puppies" was learned from Indians who dropped spoons full of cornmeal into boiling fat to create a quick snack fed to dogs to quite their barking.

Squash - The word "squash" comes from Indians of the New England area and was used as the name of a variety of related vegetables. In Italy the only American squash that became popular was the long green variety they named "zucchini" which comes from the Italian word for gourd.

Potato - Used by the peoples of both North and South America, almost 3,000 varieties of potatoes were domesticated. They varied in size, taste, color, growing conditions, etc. First shipped to Ireland during its worst famine, the potato provided Europe with its first consistent supply of cheap nutrition. The potato stored easier and kept longer than most grains that were in current use in Europe, and the vegetable eventually helped stabilize the populations of Europe. Russia became the main potato-eating nation.

Tacos, Tamales, Tortillas - Most of the foods we think of as "Mexican Food" are actually based on the original foods of the Indigenous people of the region, which are mixtures of corn or cornmeal with various meats.

Barbecue - The Taino Indians of Hispañola first demonstrated to the Spanish the process of basting meat with special sauces and then cooking it over an outdoor fire. The word "barbecue" is derived from the Taino Indian word for the process.

Amaranth - This Central American grain has the highest protein of any grain in the world. While this food is relatively unknown to most North Americans, it has been exported and widely adopted in the highlands of China, India, Tibet and Pakistan to efficiently feed the starving peoples of those lands.

Wild Rice - Cultivated by the Ojibwa and other Indians in the lakes of Minnesota and Wisconsin, wild rice thrives in the cold, whereas other types of rice must have warm, humid climates near the equator. Wild rice lies dormant in the waters of frozen lakes in the winter, and then sprouts in the spring. Wild Rice is now often mixed with white rice as a special dish to accompany delicacies.

Cajun/Creole - Essentially all of the foods that made New Orleans famous are based on foods and spices first eaten by the Indian inhabitants of the region. Indians taught French settlers which foods to eat, how to catch or grow them and how to prepare them. These foods were mixed with some additional foods brought by slaves from Africa to round out this geographically unique style of cooking.

Spices - Seasonings and spices developed by Indians of the Americas have been exported and enthusiastically adopted by peoples all over the world, including India, China, Korea, Japan and parts of Africa. Many foods and spices were transmitted throughout the nations of the British, Portuguese and Spanish empires. Surprisingly, until the introduction of American spices, Italian cuisine was rather bland. There were relatively few sauce choices to pour over their infinite varieties of pasta (which had come from China). Italian food exploded with flavor and variety when tomatoes and peppers arrived from America.

The list of seasonings with roots in the Indigenous cultures of the Americas include: allspice, cayenne, a vast variety of chiles that are the bases of spices all over the world, mints of several types, paprika, sweet peppers, pimento, Tabasco Sauce (the registered trademark of the McIlhhenny Company), vanilla and wintergreen.

Snack Foods - Potato chips, French fries, popcorn, nachos, tortilla chips, salsa, guacamole, beef jerky, peanuts, sunflower seeds, pumpkin seeds, pecans, several dried fruits, even Cracker Jacks were all American Indian originals (and Native Americans don't even get any royalties from these creations.)

Tomato - Indians developed a wide variety of colors, sizes, textures and shapes. The tomato created new taste experiences for Europeans who had been limited to sauces derived from dairy products. Each European country developed its own unique sauces, soups and other uses for this American fruit (not a vegetable).

Chocolate (cacao) - Chocolate comes from the seed of the fruit-bearing cacao plant. Extracted from the fruit, then cleaned, dried, roasted and ground. The dry powdery substance (chocolate) is the result.

"Cracker Jack" (maple syrup spread over peanuts and popcorn) - The Indians of New England and the Great Lakes region created this sweet snack food. This was stored for winter to provide a source of energy and calories when food was scarce.

Honey (wild and farmed) - Many Natives collected wild honey to use as a sweetener, but the Mayan Indians perfected the bee-keeping and honey-making process that matched anything happening in Europe.

Maple Syrup - Technology developed by the Indians of the Northeast to tap into the tree, withdraw the sap, process it into syrup and maple sugar. For a while, maple sugar provided American colonies with a good product to compete with sugarcane that was imported from Southeast Asia.

Mother Earth's Medicine Chest

While much of the world was practicing various forms of superstition and witchcraft in attempts to heal people, and European doctors used leeches, plasters, potions and crude forms of surgery, many American Indians had defined a set of naturally occurring active drugs to fight disease. European medical science praised itself as the most advanced in the world, but had no cures for malaria, smallpox, leprosy, tuberculosis, the plague or other terminal diseases. The discovery of the natural medicine chest of Native Americans formed the basis of modern medicine and pharmacology.

Quinine - Discovered and used as a traditional medicine by South American Indians as a cure for the symptoms of malaria, this substance comes from the bark of a tree. The name comes from a Quechua Indian word "quina" which means tree bark. The introduction of quinine to Europe in the 1600s marked the beginning of modern pharmacology. In the early 1800s, doctors discovered that small doses of the substance could also prevent the disease. A daily dose of "tonic" water became a popular custom among British travelers, and continues today as a popular drink.

Root Beer - Sassafras and sarsaparilla teas used by Indigenous peoples of the New World became the basis of many "miracle cures" sold by traveling medicine shows in the 1800s. Mixed with sugar, spices and carbonated water, it was sold as "Indian Root Beer" as a cure for numerous illnesses. Later, like quinine tonic, root beer came to be a drink enjoyed for refreshment, not medicinal purposes.

Ipecac - Indians of the Amazon used the roots of a tree to make this medicine as a for cure amoebic dysentery which produces high fever and bloody diarrhea. This disease is one of the world's major killers of young children in poorer parts of the world. It was also used to make a patient vomit if a poisonous substance had been swallowed. This medicine made its first European splash in France when it was used to cure dysentery in the son of King Louis XIV. Doctors all over the world still use this medicine for both children and adults.

Scurvy - Scurvy was a common disease among sailors. Europe had many plants that could easily have cured this disease, but doctors ignored these until American Indians demonstrated their usefulness. The French explorer Jacques Cartier first became aware of an Indian cure for this disease in 1535. While stranded in the frozen upper reaches of the St. Lawrence River during winter, 100 of his men came down with the disease and 75 died. Noticing that several Natives had contracted the disease, but had recovered, Cartier asked for the cure. He was shown how to make a distasteful but effective concoction from the needles of an evergreen tree (which contained massive quantities of Vitamin C, the only cure for scurvy). Every remaining man who took it recovered in 8 days.

Evergreen Pine Needles to cure scurvy

Even though Cartier wrote glowingly of this experience in his logs, it was another 200 years before European science took notice of the discovery. In 1795, The British Admiralty ordered all British ships to carry lime juice (another good source of Vitamin C) to prevent the disease. Thus, British sailors became known to the rest of the world as "limeys."

Headaches/Pain - American Indians used the inside of the bark of willows to cure aches and pains. Its active ingredient is salicin, known throughout the world today as aspirin. Arnica is also a plant-based pain killer used by Natives for bruises and sprains.

Laxative - The Natives of Northern California and Oregon gave the world what is now the most commonly used cure for constipation, named *cascara sagrada* by the Spanish, meaning "sacred bark." While there were already several remedies available in other parts of the world, none was gentler on the sufferer's intestines. Because of its bitter taste, it is often mixed with chocolate or sugar before swallowing.

Petroleum jelly - One of the most common skin ointments in the world today, it was first developed by American Indians to protect wounds, stimulate healing and keep skin moist. It was also used to lubricate the moving parts of some tools. Also known as "Indian petrolatum" in England, the product has replaced animal fat, which was used by peoples all over the world for sun protection. Since it is inorganic, however, petroleum jelly doesn't attract insects.

Bathing - Indians of many tribes bathed regularly in rivers or lakes. The Spanish outlawed this practice whenever possible because they believed it weakened the body and lead to a variety of diseases. Historically, other Europeans *rarely* engaged in this activity. The French even invented perfume to cover the stench created by their lack of bathing.

Sweats/steam baths - Tribes all over the Americas took various forms of steam baths to cleanse the body. Some were conducted ritually inside domed structures and accompanied with songs and prayers. Others were simply conducted at naturally occurring hot springs. The destruction of sweat lodges and the banning of frequent bathing by European colonizers probably contributed to the rapid spread of Old World diseases among Indians.

Coca - Indians of the Andes chewed coca leaves to refresh the mind and body and to alleviate pain and discomfort. Coca was introduced in Europe in the mid 1500s, but it wasn't until the 1850s that German chemists isolated the active ingredient and named it cocaine. Its first medical use was as anesthesia for eye and dental surgery. Today it is used by dentists the world over under the brand name Novocain. In the 1880s an American pharmacist combined coca with caffeine and the African Kola nut. The result was the stimulating drink called Coca-Cola. Later, cocaine was taken out of the drink. Unfortunately, cocaine has also become the drug of choice for many people who become addicted to it.

Other Useful Innovations

Snowshoes

American Cotton - Cotton from the New World, domesticated and grown by American Indians, grew twice as long as European and East Indian cotton. It was stronger and cheaper to grow and ship than the other varieties. For thousands of years, American Indians in various locations wove it into beautiful cloth material. As a result of this discovery, England was able to produce cotton cloth for the first time in the mid 1500's. With abundant supplies of raw cotton coming into England, the first cloth factories, called textile mills, were built. They were usually built near rivers and harnessed the power of the water wheel to operate.

Cloth Dyes - Indians of the Americas developed a complex technology for producing quality cloth dyes from a variety of plant sources. In some regions, there were up to 7 color categories with as many as 100 hues. The Indians of Mexico created beautifully brilliant red dye from the bodies of a certain insect. This dye was exported by the Spanish is great supply and traded to the British who used it for military uniforms. They were known the world over for their nickname: Redcoats. Europeans eventually adopted this color dye process.

Rubber - Natives in South America learned to extract the sap of rubber trees and cook it to make rubber balls for sporting events, raincoats and rain shoes, rubber bottles and even rubber ropes—the first bungee cords. At first, Europeans didn't see a practical use for the stuff, but in the early 1800s, Charles Goodyear found uses for it, first for bicycle tires. Soon it was mass-produced for waterproof clothing, sealing, and sports.

Asphalt/Tar - In North American, Indians from California to Pennsylvania had discovered how to apply raw asphalt, which bubbled up in pools, to baskets and cloth to make them waterproof (the way South American Indians did with rubber). Some, such as the Chumash, used it to caulk their ocean-going canoes on the West Coast. The international oil industry was launched from Pennsylvania thanks to local Indians who led oil industrialists to their open pit source for the stuff.

Snow Gear - Snowshoes were developed by Indians of the Northern and Arctic regions to walk in snow without sinking. They're made using a curved wooden frame laced with rawhide thongs. Snow goggles are made of bone, antler or ivory with a horizontal slit cut in them across the eyes to eliminate glare from the snow.

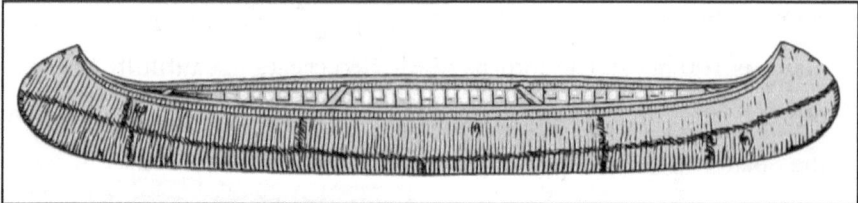

The Canoe - River and ocean-going versions were developed by Indigenous Peoples all over North and South America. The Inuit developed their own version called the Kayak. Some Central and South American Indians made boats from woven reeds. The seaworthiness of these boats was demonstrated by Thor Heyerdahl in the 1950s. He proved that Natives of the Pacific Rim could've easily sailed from South America to the Easter Islands.

Precious Metals (Gold & Silver) - America's Indians used gold and silver primarily for religious purposes, for decoration and jewelry. Many rich sources of these metals were discovered and mined by indigenous peoples. Legends and rumors of golden cities fueled the imaginations of many European explorers who marched across North, Central and South America.

These explorers enslaved indigenous people and forced them to work in the mines digging out the metals to be shipped back to Spain, Portugal or England. Vast quantities of gold and silver were shipped to Europe that sparked an economic revolution all over that continent, which in turn spread wealth to all the nations that traded with Europe.

Political Concepts

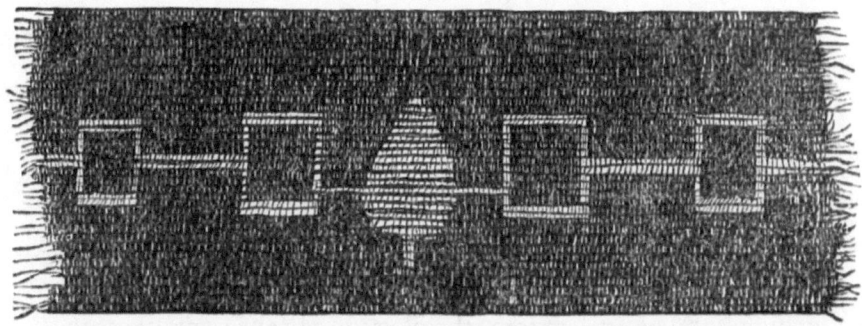

Democracy & Liberty - Many early Europeans who traveled among Native Americans and took the time to observe their social customs and lifestyles (rather than murder or enslave them as others did) noticed a remarkable quality about tribal life: personal liberty, a concept unknown to most Europeans who lived under the rule of kings whose every whim was catered to. In many tribal societies, rulers were actually servants of the people. The people lived more or less as equals, each with the freedom to follow his own vision for his life, balanced with the desire to take action, which served the good of the group. Their kinship systems served as their governments and all real property (land) was held in common. These qualities were noted in the writings of several visitors among Native Americans, including Amerigo Vespucci, for whom "America" was named. This uniquely American Indian quality was recommended by Benjamin Franklin and adopted by American colonists. It helped to fuel their cry for independence from England.
Union of States - When it came time to create the United States, the Founding Fathers faced a serious problem: how to weld thirteen separate colonies into one unified whole while still maintaining local

authority. For answers, Benjamin Franklin turned to the Iroquois League of Nations, who suggested that the colonies form a union similar to theirs. (The Iroquois Wampum Belt pictured on page 20 is a visual representation of the union of five Native nations.) The term "bury the hatchet" (meaning to come together in peace) came from the central symbol of the Iroquois League. Five different tribal nations put aside their differences and literally buried their war hatchets at the base of the Tree of Peace. Many elements of the Iroquois model found their way into the U.S. Constitution, including the federal system, the election of representatives, the separation of powers, the impeachment of unfit leaders, provisions for declaring war and making treaties, etc. None of these concepts were part of any European political system at the time. Even one of the Iroquois symbols of their union, a bundle of arrows tied together, was borrowed by our Founding Fathers. The great seal of the United States portrays an eagle clutching a cluster of thirteen arrows in one claw.

Architecture

In many parts of the United States, early settlers copied the local Native style of housing or shelter as it was the best suited to the climate and environment. In the **Southwest**, Indians used mud and straw to make adobe bricks that provided natural insulation. In the **Northeast**, Indians taught colonial villages how to surround their settlements with pointed posts buried at an outward angle in the ground for protection. On the **Great Plains**, immigrants built sod houses that were partially underground, imitating ancient Indian pit houses of the region. Along the **Northwest Coast**, Europeans adopted the long plank houses built of redwood or cedar. In World War II, army engineers copied the Iroquois longhouse design, with its integrated curved wall and ceiling shape, in the familiar **Quonset** hut. In more recent times, American engineer and designer Buckminster Fuller copied igloo and wigwam designs for his famous **Geodesic Dome** design.

Iroquois Longhouse | World War II era Quonset Hut

Transportation Routes

Today's American highway and rail systems are laid out over the American trails of the 1800s. These, in turn, were laid over the network of trails followed by early explorers and settlers. These, in turn, followed some of the original foot trails and trading routes used by American Indians who crossed long distances to trade for goods that came from other regions.

When European settlers arrived in America, they didn't have to hack their way through the wilderness or wander across the plains because Native Americans had already blazed the trails for them. Immigrants simply widened and reinforced these trails to accommodate larger, heavier vehicles.

For example, The Santa Fe Trail, which stretched from Independence, Missouri, to Santa Fe, New Mexico, was originally a Native American trail. A modern interstate highway connects these two points today.

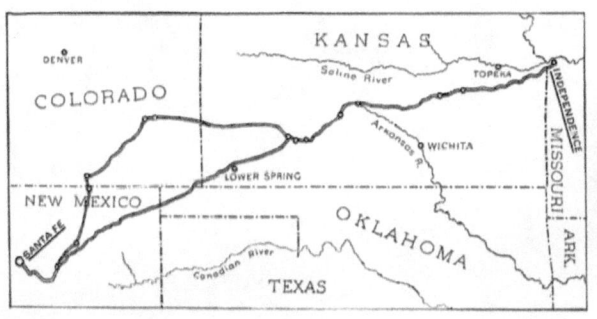

Old Santa Fe Trail from Independence, Missouri to Santa Fe, New Mexico

American Cities

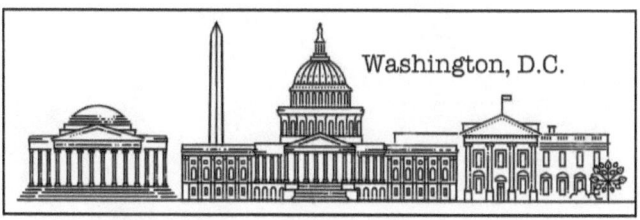
Washington, D.C.

Many of America's modern cities are built on or near original American Indian settlements, because they were the most appropriate locations for human inhabitance in the area, and entire new sites didn't have to be cleared. America has forgotten that most of its modern infrastructure has been constructed and superimposed over the original Native American layer. In fact, our nation's capital, Washington DC, was built on the site of a prosperous trading village of Native Americans who's chief was called Patawomeke, which became shortened to Potomac.

The City of Cahokia - At the height of its prosperity, the mound city of Cahokia, with its 20,000 residents, was the largest city in America north of Mexico. Located in what is now Illinois, it was larger than London, England, at the time. This ancient city sat across the Mississippi River from present day St. Louis, MO. Its central earthen pyramid is 100 feet tall, and a flat field large enough to play football on covers its top. Cahokia was the center of a vast trade network that reached into Canada and Mexico.

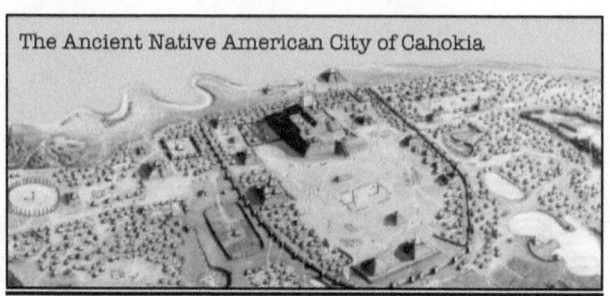
The Ancient Native American City of Cahokia

23

American Indian Words

English-speaking settlers adopted many words from Native American languages because the things they named didn't exist in Europe. Here are words from various tribes that became part of the English language:

Animals: moose, caribou, raccoon, opossum, chipmunk, barracuda, manatee, cougar, jaguar, chigger and skunk.

Foods/plants: pecan, hickory, persimmon, mahogany, mesquite, yucca, maize, squash, avocado, papaya, cassava, tapioca, succotash, potato, tomato and tobacco.

Land descriptions: bayou, savanna, pampas and Podunk.

Weather: hurricane, Chinook (winds) and blizzard.

Others: canoe, kayak, hammock, toboggan, caucus, powwow and okay.

Place Names - The names of many states, cities, rivers and other landmarks are American Indian words or Anglicized versions of Indian words, including: Massachusetts, Nantucket, Roanoke, Tallahassee, Poughkeepsie, Minnesota, Tennessee, Kansas, Dakota, Utah, Texas, Seattle, Nebraska, Alabama, Connecticut, Oregon, Mississippi, Tallahatchie, Ohio, Winnebago, Tucson, Canada, Appalachia, Wyoming. Within many states, such as California, place names were regularly taken from nearby Native villages such as Malibu, Ojai, Nipomo, Lompoc, Cuyama, Topanga, Tahunga and Cuenga.

Code Talkers & America's Wartime Victories

Native American Code Talkers of World War II

When it comes to helping our nation during wartime, American Indian words have played huge roles in America's ability to defeat its enemies. Almost everyone has heard of the Navajo Code Talkers of World War II, but few know of the 30 other tribal languages used to send coded wartime messages during <u>both</u> World War I and World War II.

Even though American Indians weren't allowed to become citizens of the U.S. until 1924, thousands enlisted in the military at the outbreak of WWI. Soldiers from dozens of tribes shipped off to Europe and fought valiantly on many fronts. However, the Germans were experts at tapping into Allied phone lines and breaking the codes used to communicate military maneuvers to our men on the front lines. That ability resulted in defeat after defeat as the enemy always knew where and when to strike.

America was losing that war until a clever bunch of Choctaws got the bright idea of using their language as a means of sending coded communications. Since nothing else had worked, the allied leaders agreed to give it a try. A fluent Choctaw speaker was stationed at headquarters while others were stationed out in field positions.

When the Germans were unable to decode the first test messages using the Choctaw language, U.S. military command knew it was on to something big. Other Native languages were also used in that war, and none of those were ever deciphered by the enemy.

The successful use of Native languages in that war led to a more sophisticated application of the process during WWII. The Marine Corps enlisted several groups of fluent Navajo speakers for the fight against Japan in the Pacific. The first batch of Navajo recruits devised the code using common everyday Navajo words to stand for a large variety of military items and actions. For example, the Navajo word for potato became the coded word for hand grenade. A submarine became the "iron fish." In addition, Comanche code talkers developed a similar code for use with the Army in the war against Hitler in Europe. Thus "pregnant woman" became the phrase for identifying a bomber airplane.

Code Talkers from 33 tribes were finally and belatedly recognized for their service with Congressional Medals of Honor bestowed in 2013.

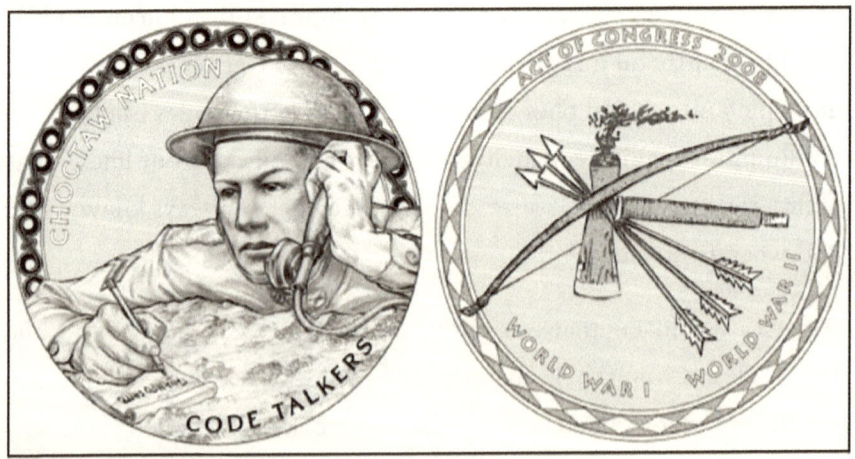

American Indians, Animals and the Environment

The Forests & Prairies — Native Americans often managed the prairies and forests using a technique known as the "controlled burn" to clear dense underbrush. This process has many advantages. It clears away parasitic plants that choke and kill large growth trees, increases grazing areas for herds of buffalo and other large animals, minimizes the danger from large uncontrolled fires caused by lightning, reduces the number of irritating insects, drives off snakes, provides more room for large trees to grow and generally helps both land and people thrive. This natural balance was destroyed when American Indians were displaced and Euro-American settlers, unfamiliar with forest and range management, moved in. Natives even taught Europeans how to use 'backfires" to control and contain large forest fires, a technique commonly used today.

Bison (Buffalo) - The Bison or American Buffalo once roamed the American Plains in huge numbers, as many as 70 million in some estimates. They were perfectly adapted to the plains, and their existence kept the environment in balance. Many Native communities depended on the buffalo for their very lives. Religious ceremonies honored the spirit and power of the animal. Many tribes followed the migrations of buffalo herds and hunted them during certain seasons of the year. But Indians usually killed only as many bison as they needed for survival, and used every part of the animal's body for food, shelter, clothing and utensils. Indians even thanked the buffalo's spirit for its sacrifice so that the people could live.

When non-Indian settlers moved into the area in the 1800s, they ignored the buffalo as a food source and brought beef cattle and farming in. Then In the mid-1800s, the army ordered the slaughter of herds of buffalo as a way to defeat the Indians, force them to move to reservations, and to make way for more cattle. By the end of the 1800s, there may have been as few as 100 of the animals left alive, according to some estimates.

Fortunately, today the Buffalo is making a strong comeback, thanks to the efforts of the Native Inter-tribal Bison Cooperative. Recognizing the economic benefits and the spiritual symbolism that the buffalo bring to Indian people, several tribes have established their own herds.

Salmon - In the Northwest United States, in the areas that are now Washington and Oregon, indigenous peoples fished for Salmon in rivers, such as the Columbia, for centuries, maintaining a careful balance with nature. The salmon was so important to their lives that many tribes in the area honored the fish with annual ceremonies and dances.

To catch the fish, Indians built large platforms on stilts that jutted out over the water, and from those platforms, they netted salmon as they swam upstream. Of course, they only took as many fish from the water as they needed to survive.

But in the mid 1900s, dams were built in several places along these rivers to create lakes and to generate electricity. These dams blocked the path the salmon took to swim upstream to lay their eggs.

As a result, few fish were able to lay their eggs and the salmon population began to severely dwindle.

To make matters worse, the government made it illegal for people, including Indian people, to fish for salmon. Many Indians didn't have any other way to make a living or get food.

To help solve the problem, the Northwest Indian Fisheries Commission was created in 1974 to govern fishing in the area. As a result, salmon and other native fish once again flourish.

Games and Sports

Indigenous communities of the Americas invented many different types of games and sports competitions, some of which found their way to Europe to be modified and adopted there.

Archery – Of course, archery was practiced by many different nations and cultures around the world. In America, not only was it used for hunting and warfare, but also as competitive sport for Native youth to develop skills that would be needed in adulthood.

LaCrosse – This competitive team sport is probably best known to most people. Tribes in Canada and the norther regions of the U.S. played this using a single long stick with a basket-like net at the end. French colonists observed the game in America, transported it back to their home and gave it the name LaCrosse, meaning "hooked stick." Southern tribes in the U.S. use two sticks in the game, calling the game simply "stickball." Games were sometimes played on huge fields, with hundreds of players, and could settle disputes between communities. This version was known as the "Little Brother of War."

Traditional LaCrosse and Stickball Players

Shinny — This team sport is similar to hockey accept that it is played on solid ground instead of ice, and a ball is used instead of a puck. Different versions of the game were played traditionally by a variety of tribes. This sport is believed to be the forerunner of hockey.

Shinny Players

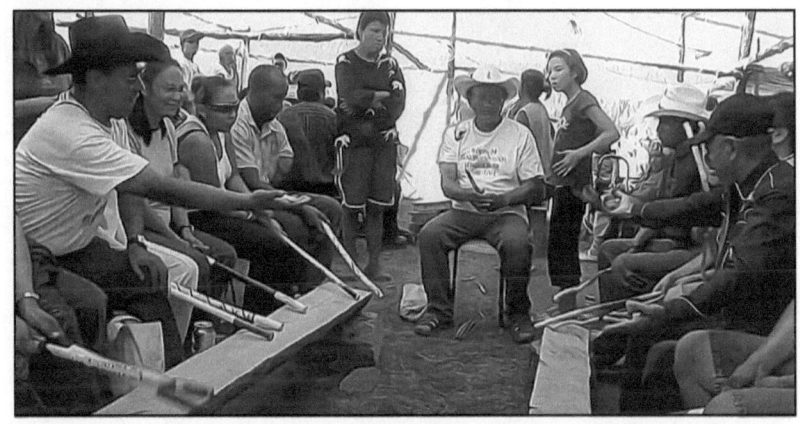

Stick Game/Hand Game/Bone Game – Played by tribes all across North America, this guessing game is still played today. The set-up calls for two teams that face each other. One team is the "hiding team" and the other is the "guessing team." The objects being hidden are called "bones" and might be made from animal bone or carved from wood. A set of sticks are used to keep score. In some versions, players sit on the ground. In other versions, they are seated, usually with a log or flat wooden surface in front of them. A single game can last hours as the two teams take turns doing the guessing and hiding.

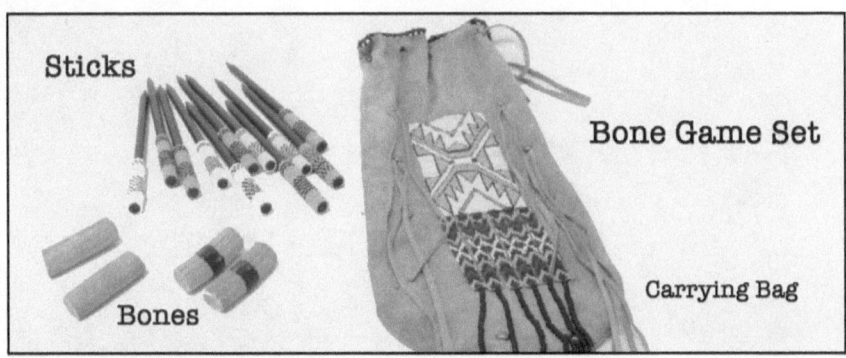

Bibliography

1. ***Encyclopedia of American Indian Contributions to the World*** Emory Dean and Kay Marie Porterfield; Facts on File, Inc., 2002.

2. ***Indian Givers: How the Indians of the Americas Transformed the World.*** Jack Weatherford; Crown Publishing, 1988.

3. ***Native Roots: How the Indians Enriched America*** Jack Weatherford; Fawcett Book Group, 1992.

4. ***Savages and Civilization: Who Will Survive*** Jack Weatherford; Crown Publishing, 1993.

5. ***The Language of Victory: The Code Talkers of WWI & WWII*** (book and video) Gary Robinson, Tribal Eye Productions, 2014.

6. ***Forgotten Founders: How the American Indian Helped Shape Democracy.*** Bruce E. Johansen; Harvard Common Press, 1982.

7. ***Little Brother of War.*** Gary Robinson; Native Voices Books.

8. ***A Native American Thought of It***. Rocky Landon; Annick Press.

ABOUT THE AUTHOR

Gary Robinson, a writer, artist and filmmaker of Choctaw and Cherokee Indian descent, has spent more than thirty years working with American Indian communities to tell the historical and contemporary stories of Native peoples in all forms of media.

His television work has aired on PBS, Turner Broadcasting, Ovation Network, and others. His non-fiction books, From Warriors to Soldiers and The Language of Victory, reveal little-known aspects of American Indian service in the U.S. military from the Revolutionary War to modern times.

He is also the author of several teen novels in the *PathFinders* series published by Native Voices Books. This unique series features Native American teen main characters who go on adventures and rediscover the value of their own tribal identities. (www.NativeVoicesBooks.com)

His children's books include Native American Night Before Christmas, published by Native Voices Books.

He lives in rural central California. More information about the author can be found at www.tribaleyeproductions.com. Follow him on Facebook at www.facebook.com/tribaleyepro.

www.ingramcontent.com/pod-product-compliance
Lightning Source LLC
Chambersburg PA
CBHW020703300426
44112CB00007B/505